Entertainment Directory

BERLIN
RESTAURANT
GUIDE 2015

RESTAURANTS, BARS & CAFES

★★★★★

The Most Positively
Reviewed and Recommended
Restaurants in the City

EGP
Editorial

BERLIN RESTAURANT GUIDE 2015
Restaurants, Bars & Cafés

© Matthew H. Gundrey, 2015
© E.G.P. Editorial, 2015

Web: http://www.EGPGuides.com/

Printed in USA.

ISBN-13: 978-1505443394
ISBN-10: 1505443393

BERLIN RESTAURANT GUIDE 2015

Restaurants, Bars and Cafés in Berlin

This directory is dedicated to Berlin Business Owners and Managers who provide the experience that the locals and tourists enjoy. Thanks you very much for all that you do and thank for being the "People Choice".

Thanks to everyone that posts their reviews online and the amazing reviews sites that make our life easier.

The places listed in this book are the most positively reviewed and recommended by locals and travelers from around the world.

Thank you for your time and enjoy the directory that is designed with locals and tourist in mind!

TOP 500
RESTAURANTS
Ranked from #1 to #500

#1
Figl
Cuisines: Pizza, German
Average price: €8-20
Area: Kreuzberg
Address: Urbanstr. 47
10967 Berlin Germany
Phone: +49 30 72290850

#2
I-Ke-Su
Cuisines: Japanese, Sushi Bar
Average price: €8-20
Area: Wilmersdorf
Address: Uhlandstr. 157
10719 Berlin Germany
Phone: +49 30 88910939

#3
Trattoria La Terrazza
Cuisines: Italian
Average price: €8-20
Area: Neukölln
Address: Steinbockstr. 20
12057 Berlin Germany
Phone: +49 30 68053745

#4
Beakers
Cuisines: Breakfast & Brunch, Cafe
Average price: €8-20
Area: Prenzlauer Berg
Address: Dunckerstr. 69
10437 Berlin Germany
Phone: +49 30 55575850

#5
Peking Ente
Cuisines: Chinese, Asian Fusion
Average price: €8-20
Area: Mitte
Address: Voßstr. 1
10117 Berlin Germany
Phone: +49 30 2294523

#6
Fassbender & Rausch
Cuisines: Chocolatiers, Desserts
Average price: €21-40
Area: Mitte
Address: Charlottenstr. 60
10117 Berlin Germany
Phone: +49 30 20458440

#7
Hoan Kiem
Cuisines: Vietnamese
Average price: Under €7
Area: Tiergarten
Address: Jonasstraße 4
10551 Berlin Germany
Phone: +49 30 3963632

#8
Buscaglione
Cuisines: Coffee & Tea, Italian, Tapas
Average price: €8-20
Area: Mitte
Address: Rochstr. 3
10178 Berlin Germany
Phone: +49 30 49353111

#9
Mutti Hausmannskost de Luxe
Cuisines: German
Average price: €21-40
Area: Kreuzberg
Address: Großbeerenstr. 36
10965 Berlin Germany
Phone: +49 30 74398945

#10
1900 Cafe Bistro
Cuisines: Cafe
Average price: €8-20
Area: Wilmersdorf
Address: Knesebeckstr.76
10623 Berlin Germany
Phone: +49 30 88715871

#11
Viasko
Cuisines: Bar, Vegan
Average price: €8-20
Area: Kreuzberg
Address: Erkelenzdamm 49
10999 Berlin Germany
Phone: +49 30 88499785

#12
Louise Chérie Café
Cuisines: Cafe
Average price: €8-20
Area: Friedrichshain
Address: Grünberger Str. 91
10245 Berlin Germany
Phone: +49 30 68070609

#13
Traube
Cuisines: Wine Bar, German
Average price: €21-40
Area: Mitte
Address: Reinhardtstr. 33
10117 Berlin Germany
Phone: +49 30 27879393

#14
Cocolo Ramen
Cuisines: Japanese
Average price: €8-20
Area: Mitte
Address: Gipsstr. 3
10119 Berlin Germany
Phone: +49 172 3047584

#15
Zur Bratpfanne
Cuisines: Cafe
Average price: €8-20
Area: Steglitz
Address: Schloßstr/ Ecke Kielerstr.
12163 Berlin Germany
Phone: +49 30 79788360

#16
Bao
Cuisines: Vietnamese
Average price: €8-20
Area: Steglitz
Address: Hindenburgdamm 57a
12203 Berlin Germany
Phone: +49 30 83203483

#17
Paris Moskau
Cuisines: International
Average price: €21-40
Area: Tiergarten
Address: Alt Moabit 141
10557 Berlin Germany
Phone: +49 30 3942081

#18
Güllü Lahmacun
Cuisines: Turkish, Delicatessen
Average price: Under €7
Area: Tiergarten
Address: Perlebergerstr. 56
10559 Berlin Germany
Phone: +49 30 51736076

#19
Chay Viet
Cuisines: Vegetarian
Average price: Under €7
Area: Mitte
Address: Brunnenstr. 164
10119 Berlin Germany
Phone: +49 30 48494554

#20
Rogacki
Cuisines: Delicatessen, Fast Food
Average price: €21-40
Area: Charlottenburg
Address: Wilmersdorfer Str. 145
10585 Berlin Germany
Phone: +49 30 3438250

#21
Izmir Koftecisi
Cuisines: Turkish, Kebab
Average price: Under €7
Area: Kreuzberg
Address: Reichenbergerstr. 10
10999 Berlin Germany
Phone: +49 6159 266

#22
Steakhouse ASADOR
Cuisines: Steakhouse, International
Average price: €8-20
Area: Kreuzberg
Address: Wilhelmstr. 22
10963 Berlin Germany
Phone: +49 30 25931818

#23
Pizza Nostra
Cuisines: Pizza, Italian
Average price: €8-20
Area: Prenzlauer Berg
Address: Lychener Str. 2
10437 Berlin Germany
Phone: +49 30 41717000

#24
Bellas Artes
Cuisines: Spanish, Tapas Bar
Average price: €8-20
Area: Wilmersdorf
Address: Pfalzburger Str. 72a
10719 Berlin Germany
Phone: +49 30 88680541

#25
Gasthaus Alt Wien
Cuisines: Austrian
Average price: €21-40
Area: Prenzlauer Berg
Address: Hufelandstr. 22
10407 Berlin Germany
Phone: +49 30 70129610

#26
Frau Bäckerin
Cuisines: Cafe
Average price: Under €7
Area: Schöneberg
Address: Eisenacher Str. 40
10781 Berlin Germany
Phone: +49 30 68074565

#27
Rembrandt-Burger
Cuisines: Burgers
Average price: €8-20
Area: Friedrichshain
Address: Richard-Sorge-Str. 21
10249 Berlin Germany
Phone: +49 30 89997296

#28
Reinstoff
Cuisines: European
Average price: Above €41
Area: Mitte
Address: Schlegelstr. 26c
10115 Berlin Germany
Phone: +49 30 30881214

#29
Matreshka
Cuisines: Russian
Average price: Under €7
Area: Friedrichshain
Address: Boxhagener Str. 60
10245 Berlin Germany
Phone: +49 163 9870767

#30
Facil
Cuisines: German
Average price: €21-40
Area: Tiergarten
Address: Potsdamer Str. 3
10785 Berlin Germany
Phone: +49 30 590051234

#31
Café Finovo
Cuisines: Cafe
Average price: Under €7
Area: Schöneberg
Address: Großgörschenstr. 12-14
10829 Berlin Germany
Phone: +49 30 20615520

#32
Restaurant Bastard
Cuisines: International,
Breakfast & Brunch
Average price: €8-20
Area: Kreuzberg
Address: Reichenberger Str. 122
10999 Berlin Germany
Phone: +49 30 54821866

#33
L'Escargot
Cuisines: Mediterranean
Average price: €21-40
Area: Wedding
Address: Brüsseler Str. 39
13353 Berlin Germany
Phone: +49 30 4531563

#34
Gabi's Imbiss
Cuisines: Food Truck
Average price: €8-20
Area: Wilmersdorf
Address: auf verschiedenen
Wochenmärkten,10709 Berlin Germany
Phone: +49 175 8777550

#35
Madang
Cuisines: Korean
Average price: €8-20
Area: Kreuzberg
Address: Gneisenaustr. 8
10961 Berlin Germany
Phone: +49 30 48827992

#36
Dolores
Cuisines: Mexican, Vegetarian, Vegan
Average price: €8-20
Area: Mitte
Address: Rosa-Luxemburg-Str. 7
10178 Berlin Germany
Phone: +49 30 28099597

#37
Focaccia, Pasta & Pizza
Cuisines: Italian, Pizza
Average price: Under €7
Area: Tiergarten
Address: Alt-Moabit 51
10555 Berlin Germany
Phone: +49 176 26123823

#38
Saigon Today
Cuisines: Asian Fusion, Vietnamese
Average price: Under €7
Area: Wilmersdorf
Address: Wilmersdorfer Str. 69
10629 Berlin Germany
Phone: +49 30 32766081

#39
Tiergartenquelle
Cuisines: German, Pub
Average price: €8-20
Area: Tiergarten
Address: Bachstr. / S-Bahnbogen 482
10555 Berlin Germany
Phone: +49 30 3927615

#40
Weingalerie und Café NÖ!
Cuisines: Wine Bar, German, Mediterranean
Average price: €8-20
Area: Mitte
Address: Glinkastr. 23
10117 Berlin Germany
Phone: +49 30 2010871

#41
Restaurant Alt Luxemburg
Cuisines: Seafood, Mediterranean
Average price: €21-40
Area: Charlottenburg
Address: Windscheidstr. 31
10627 Berlin Germany
Phone: +49 30 3238730

#42
Panoramapunkt & Panoramacafé
Cuisines: Cafe
Average price: €8-20
Area: Tiergarten
Address: Potsdamer Platz 1
10785 Berlin Germany
Phone: +49 30 25937080

#43
Cô Cô Bánh Mì Deli
Cuisines: Vietnamese, Sandwiches
Average price: €8-20
Area: Mitte
Address: Rosenthaler Str. 2
10119 Berlin Germany
Phone: +49 30 24630595

#44
Gingi's Izakaya
Cuisines: Sushi Bar, Japanese
Average price: €8-20
Area: Prenzlauer Berg
Address: Rykestr. 45
10405 Berlin Germany
Phone: +49 30 44049397

#45
Pierogarnia
Cuisines: Polish
Average price: Under €7
Area: Wedding
Address: Turiner Str. 21
13347 Berlin Germany
Phone: +49 30 89626927

#46
SAIGON and more ...
Cuisines: Vietnamese
Average price: €8-20
Area: Schöneberg
Address: Geisbergstr. 12
10777 Berlin Germany
Phone: +49 30 23626090

#47
Mio
Cuisines: Bistro
Average price: €8-20
Area: Friedrichshain
Address: Samariterstr. 36
10247 Berlin Germany
Phone: +49 30 48624173

#48
Déjà Vu
Cuisines: French
Average price: €8-20
Area: Pankow
Address: Binzstr. 52-53
13189 Berlin Germany
Phone: +49 30 47036710

#49
Clärchens Ballhaus
Cuisines: Italian, German
Average price: €8-20
Area: Mitte
Address: Auguststr. 24
10117 Berlin Germany
Phone: +49 30 44327729

#50
Aunt Benny
Cuisines: Breakfast & Brunch
Average price: €8-20
Area: Friedrichshain
Address: Oderstr. 7
10247 Berlin Germany
Phone: +49 30 66405300

#51
Barcomi's Deli
Cuisines: Cafe
Average price: €8-20
Area: Mitte
Address: Sophienstr. 21
10178 Berlin Germany
Phone: +49 30 28598363

#52
Zweistrom
Cuisines: Arabian
Average price: Under €7
Area: Prenzlauer Berg
Address: Kollwitzstr. 104
10435 Berlin Germany
Phone: +49 1573 1441613

#53
Brechts Restaurant
Cuisines: German, Austrian
Average price: €21-40
Area: Mitte
Address: Schiffbauerdamm 6-7
10117 Berlin Germany
Phone: +49 30 28598585

#54
Schnitzelei
Cuisines: German, Austrian
Average price: €8-20
Area: Charlottenburg
Address: Röntgenstr. 7
10587 Berlin Germany
Phone: +49 30 34702777

#55
Proviant
Cuisines: Specialty Food,
Breakfast & Brunch
Average price: €8-20
Area: Friedrichshain
Address: Wühlischstr. 39a
10245 Berlin Germany
Phone: +49 30 29001174

#56
Al-Andalos
Cuisines: Kebab, Lebanese
Average price: Under €7
Area: Neukölln
Address: Sonnenallee 40
12045 Berlin Germany
Phone: +49 174 2621415

#57
City Chicken
Cuisines: Fast Food, Brasseries
Average price: €8-20
Area: Tempelhof
Address: Tempelhofer Damm 149
12099 Berlin Germany
Phone: +49 30 75687999

#58
CROSS Finest Deli
Cuisines: Mediterranean, Cafe
Average price: €8-20
Area: Charlottenburg
Address: Else-Ury-Bogen 597
10623 Berlin Germany
Phone: +49 30 31013100

#59
Eetcafé Linda Carrell
Cuisines: Cafe
Average price: €8-20
Area: Prenzlauer Berg
Address: Rhinower Str. 3
10437 Berlin Germany
Phone: +49 30 60922350

#60
Gaststätte Oderquelle
Cuisines: German
Average price: €21-40
Area: Prenzlauer Berg
Address: Oderberger Str. 27
10435 Berlin Germany
Phone: +49 30 44008080

#61
Musashi
Cuisines: Sushi Bar, Japanese
Average price: €8-20
Area: Kreuzberg
Address: Kottbusser Damm 102
10967 Berlin Germany
Phone: +49 30 6932042

#62
Trattoria del Corso
Cuisines: Italian
Average price: €8-20
Area: Schöneberg
Address: Hauptstr. 70
12159 Berlin Germany
Phone: +49 30 85401459

#63
Imbiss 204
Cuisines: German
Average price: Under €7
Area: Prenzlauer Berg
Address: Prenzlauer Allee 204
10405 Berlin Germany
Phone: +49 30 24038543

#64
Habba Habba
Cuisines: Fast Food
Average price: €8-20
Area: Prenzlauer Berg
Address: Kastanienallee 15
10435 Berlin Germany
Phone: +49 30 36745726

#65
Berkis
Cuisines: Greek
Average price: €8-20
Area: Schöneberg
Address: Winterfeldtstr. 45
10781 Berlin Germany
Phone: +49 30 77900402

#66
La Pausa
Cuisines: Italian, Pizza
Average price: Under €7
Area: Mitte
Address: Torstr. 125
10119 Berlin Germany
Phone: +49 30 24083108

#67
Hostaria La buona forchetta
Cuisines: Italian
Average price: €8-20
Area: Kreuzberg
Address: Graefestraße 83
10967 Berlin Germany
Phone: +49 30 22327119

#68
Bejte Ethiopia
Cuisines: Ethiopian, African
Average price: €8-20
Area: Schöneberg
Address: Zietenstr. 8
10783 Berlin Germany
Phone: +49 30 2625933

#69
Garda Pizza
Cuisines: Pizza
Average price: Under €7
Area: Schöneberg
Address: Crellestr. 48
10827 Berlin Germany
Phone: +49 30 78097970

#70
First Floor
Cuisines: German
Average price: Above €41
Area: Wilmersdorf
Address: Budapester Str. 45
10787 Berlin Germany
Phone: +49 30 25021020

#71
Marjellchen
Cuisines: German
Average price: €8-20
Area: Wilmersdorf
Address: Mommsenstr. 9
10629 Berlin Germany
Phone: +49 30 8832676

#72
Taverna Ousies
Cuisines: Greek
Average price: €8-20
Area: Schöneberg
Address: Grunewaldstr. 16
10823 Berlin Germany
Phone: +49 30 2167957

#73
East Restuarant
Cuisines: Chinese
Average price: €8-20
Area: Charlottenburg
Address: Grolmanstr. 21
10623 Berlin Germany
Phone: +49 30 60940932

#74
Block House
Cuisines: Steakhouse
Average price: €21-40
Area: Mitte
Address: Friedrichstr. 100
10117 Berlin Germany
Phone: +49 30 20074377

#75
Maultaschen Manufaktur
Cuisines: German
Average price: €8-20
Area: Tiergarten
Address: Lützowstr. 22
10785 Berlin Germany
Phone: +49 176 63846563

#76
Sorsi e Morsi
Cuisines: Italian, Specialty Food
Average price: €8-20
Area: Prenzlauer Berg
Address: Marienburger Str. 10
10405 Berlin Germany
Phone: +49 30 44038216

#77
Le Cochon Bourgeois
Cuisines: French
Average price: €21-40
Area: Kreuzberg
Address: Fichtestr. 24
10967 Berlin Germany
Phone: +49 30 6930101

#78
Mercan
Cuisines: Turkish
Average price: Under €7
Area: Kreuzberg
Address: Wiener Str. 10
10999 Berlin Germany
Phone: +49 30 61285841

#79
Napoljonska
Cuisines: Desserts, Breakfast & Brunch
Average price: €8-20
Area: Mitte
Address: Kastanienallee 43
10119 Berlin Germany
Phone: +49 163 8286330

#80
Balthazar
Cuisines: European
Average price: €21-40
Area: Wilmersdorf
Address: Kurfürstendamm 160
10709 Berlin Germany
Phone: +49 30 89408477

#81
China Club
Cuisines: Chinese, Lounge
Average price: Above €41
Area: Mitte
Address: Behrensstr.72
10117 Berlin Germany
Phone: +49 30 209120

#82
BASE_Camp
Cuisines: Cafe, Mobile Phones
Average price: €8-20
Area: Mitte
Address: Mittelstr. 51
10117 Berlin Germany
Phone: +49 30 34620749

#83
Pastapresti
Cuisines: Italian
Average price: €8-20
Area: Friedrichshain
Address: Wühlischstr. 39a
10247 Berlin Germany
Phone: +49 30 29047938

#84
Brunello
Cuisines: Italian
Average price: €21-40
Area: Charlottenburg
Address: Knesebeckstr. 18
10623 Berlin Germany
Phone: +49 30 3129381

#85
Restaurant La Tettoia
Cuisines: Italian
Average price: €8-20
Area: Tiergarten
Address: Waldstr. 55
10551 Berlin Germany
Phone: +49 30 3963147

#86
Westberlin
Cuisines: Desserts, Cafe
Average price: €8-20
Area: Kreuzberg
Address: Friedrichstr. 215
10969 Berlin Germany
Phone: +49 30 25922745

#87
Brasserie La Bonne Franquette
Cuisines: French
Average price: €21-40
Area: Mitte
Address: Chausseestr. 110
10115 Berlin Germany
Phone: +49 30 94405363

#88
Dada Falafel
Cuisines: Moroccan, Middle Eastern
Average price: €8-20
Area: Mitte
Address: Linienstr. 132
10115 Berlin Germany
Phone: +49 179 5105435

#89
Fischers Fritz
Cuisines: German, Seafood
Average price: Above €41
Area: Mitte
Address: Charlottenstr. 49
10117 Berlin Germany
Phone: +49 30 20336363

#90
Vego Foodworld
Cuisines: Vegan, Vegetarian
Average price: Under €7
Area: Prenzlauer Berg
Address: Lychener Str. 63
10437 Berlin Germany
Phone: +49 30 30347975

#91
Der Fischladen
Cuisines: Seafood, Fishmonger
Average price: €8-20
Area: Prenzlauer Berg
Address: Schönhauser Allee 128
10437 Berlin Germany
Phone: +49 30 40005612

#92
Trattoria Libau
Cuisines: Italian, Pizza
Average price: €8-20
Area: Friedrichshain
Address: Libauer Str. 10
10245 Berlin Germany
Phone: +49 30 25768529

#93
Gasthaus Gottlob
Cuisines: Desserts, Mediterranean, Breakfast & Brunch
Average price: €8-20
Area: Schöneberg
Address: Akazienstr. 17
10823 Berlin Germany
Phone: +49 30 78708095

#94
Weltrestaurant Markthalle
Cuisines: German, Breakfast & Brunch
Average price: €8-20
Area: Kreuzberg
Address: Pücklerstr. 34
10997 Berlin Germany
Phone: +49 30 6175502

#95
La Raclette
Cuisines: French, Cocktail Bar
Average price: €21-40
Area: Kreuzberg
Address: Lausitzer Str. 34
10999 Berlin Germany
Phone: +49 30 61287121

#96
Restaurant 44
Cuisines: European, German
Average price: €21-40
Area: Wilmersdorf
Address: Augsburger Str. 44
10789 Berlin Germany
Phone: +49 30 220102288

#97
The King of Falafel
Mos Kleiner Imbiss
Cuisines: Middle Eastern, Vegan
Average price: Under €7
Area: Kreuzberg
Address: Urbanstr. 68
10967 Berlin Germany
Phone: +49 30 74073666

#98
Uhlala
Cuisines: Ice Cream, Cafe
Average price: Under €7
Area: Wilmersdorf
Address: Uhlandstr. 168
10719 Berlin Germany
Phone: +49 178 3742662

#99
Atame Tapas Bar
Cuisines: Bar, Tapas Bar
Average price: €21-40
Area: Mitte
Address: Dircksenstr. 40
10178 Berlin Germany
Phone: +49 30 28042560

#100
Tônis
Cuisines: Vietnamese
Average price: Under €7
Area: Tiergarten
Address: Huttenstr. 68
10553 Berlin Germany
Phone: +49 30 34357754

#101
Kopps
Cuisines: Vegan
Average price: €21-40
Area: Mitte
Address: Linienstr.94
10115 Berlin Germany
Phone: +49 30 43209775

#102
Sushi Bar Ky
Cuisines: Japanese, Sushi Bar
Average price: €8-20
Area: Prenzlauer Berg
Address: Oderberger Str. 40
10435 Berlin Germany
Phone: +49 30 32519425

#103
Cocoro
Cuisines: Japanese
Average price: Under €7
Area: Kreuzberg
Address: Mehringdamm 64
10961 Berlin Germany
Phone: +49 30 81494329

#104
Curry Baude
Cuisines: Curry Sausage, Fast Food
Average price: Under €7
Area: Wedding
Address: Badstr. 1-5
13357 Berlin Germany
Phone: +49 30 4941414

#105
Fünf & Sechzig
Cuisines: German
Average price: €8-20
Area: Wedding
Address: Torfstraße 9
13353 Berlin Germany
Phone: +49 30 30606000

#106
Café Jacques
Cuisines: French, Middle Eastern
Average price: €8-20
Area: Neukölln
Address: Maybachufer 14
12047 Berlin Germany
Phone: +49 30 6941048

#107
Via Lattea
Cuisines: Italian
Average price: €8-20
Area: Prenzlauer Berg
Address: Prenzlauer Allee 41
10405 Berlin Germany
Phone: +49 4401 7237

#108
Volt
Cuisines: German, International
Average price: €21-40
Area: Kreuzberg
Address: Paul-Lincke-Ufer 21
10999 Berlin Germany
Phone: +49 30 338402320

#109
Estiatorion Jevssis
Cuisines: Greek
Average price: Above €41
Area: Steglitz
Address: Lepsiusstr. 45
12163 Berlin Germany
Phone: +49 30 79747669

#110
Sadhu
Cuisines: Pakistani, Indian
Average price: €8-20
Area: Kreuzberg
Address: Falckensteinstr. 41
10997 Berlin Germany
Phone: +49 30 76211720

#111
E.T.A.
Cuisines: European
Average price: €21-40
Area: Kreuzberg
Address: Yorckstr. 83
10965 Berlin Germany
Phone: +49 30 78098809

#112
Royal Garden
Cuisines: Chinese, Mongolian
Average price: €8-20
Area: Steglitz
Address: Osdorfer Str. 26
12207 Berlin Germany
Phone: +49 30 81852332

#113
Rutz
Cuisines: European
Average price: €21-40
Area: Mitte
Address: Chausseestr. 8
10115 Berlin Germany
Phone: +49 30 24628760

#114
Karun Bistro 1
Cuisines: Arabian, Middle Eastern
Average price: Under €7
Area: Charlottenburg
Address: Pestalozzistr. 26
10627 Berlin Germany
Phone: +49 30 31519715

#115
Restaurant El Borriquito
Cuisines: Spanish
Average price: €8-20
Area: Charlottenburg
Address: Wielandstr. 6
10625 Berlin Germany
Phone: +49 30 3129929

#116
Zula
Cuisines: Vegetarian, Middle Eastern
Average price: €8-20
Area: Prenzlauer Berg
Address: Husemannstr. 10
10435 Berlin Germany
Phone: +49 30 41715100

#117
Entrecôte
Cuisines: French, Brasseries
Average price: €21-40
Area: Mitte
Address: Schützenstr. 5
10117 Berlin Germany
Phone: +49 30 20165496

#118
BBI Berlinburger International
Cuisines: Burgers, Fast Food
Average price: €8-20
Area: Neukölln
Address: Pannierstr. 5
12047 Berlin Germany
Phone: +49 178 5407409

#119
Die Legende Von Paula & Ben
Cuisines: Wine Bar, Tapas
Average price: €8-20
Area: Kreuzberg
Address: Gneisenaustr. 58
10961 Berlin Germany
Phone: +49 30 28034400

#120
Brasserie am Gendarmenmarkt
Cuisines: Brasseries
Average price: €21-40
Area: Mitte
Address: Taubenstr. 30
10117 Berlin Germany
Phone: +49 30 20453501

#121
Pasternak
Cuisines: Russian
Average price: €8-20
Area: Prenzlauer Berg
Address: Knaackstr. 22
10405 Berlin Germany
Phone: +49 30 4413399

#122
Vau
Cuisines: German, European
Average price: Above €41
Area: Mitte
Address: Jägerstr. 54
10117 Berlin Germany
Phone: +49 30 2029730

#123
Il Santo - Caffé-Osteria
Cuisines: Coffee & Tea
Average price: €8-20
Area: Mitte
Address: Elisabethkirchstr. 1
10115 Berlin Germany
Phone: +49 30 44033760

#124
Toca Rouge
Cuisines: Chinese
Average price: €8-20
Area: Mitte
Address: Torstr. 195
10115 Berlin Germany
Phone: +49 30 84712142

#125
Lei e Lui
Cuisines: Mediterranean, Oriental
Average price: €8-20
Area: Tiergarten
Address: Wilsnacker Str. 61
10559 Berlin Germany
Phone: +49 30 30208890

#126
Die Löffelei - Coffee & Soup
Cuisines: Cafe, Bistro, Soup
Average price: €8-20
Area: Tiergarten
Address: Potsdamer Straße 73
10785 Berlin Germany
Phone: +49 30 26394898

#127
Tiki Heart Café
Cuisines: Burgers, Lounge, Hawaiian
Average price: €8-20
Area: Kreuzberg
Address: Wiener Str. 20
10999 Berlin Germany
Phone: +49 30 61074703

#128
Sasaya
Cuisines: Japanese
Average price: €8-20
Area: Prenzlauer Berg
Address: Lychener str. 50
10437 Berlin Germany
Phone: +49 30 44717721

#129
Nachtigall Imbiss
Cuisines: Middle Eastern
Average price: Under €7
Area: Kreuzberg
Address: Ohlauer Straße 10
10999 Berlin Germany
Phone: +49 30 6117115

#130
AmmAmma
Cuisines: Indian
Average price: Under €7
Area: Kreuzberg
Address: Urbanstr. 28a
10967 Berlin Germany
Phone: +49 30 74073516

#131
Lac Viet
Cuisines: Vietnamese
Average price: Under €7
Area: Steglitz
Address: Rheinstr. 50
12161 Berlin Germany
Phone: +49 30 84183160

#132
Gel Gör Inegöl Köfteci
Cuisines: Turkish
Average price: Under €7
Area: Neukölln
Address: Kottbusser Damm 80
10967 Berlin Germany
Phone: +49 30 69582753

#133
Miss Saigon
Cuisines: Vietnamese
Average price: Under €7
Area: Kreuzberg
Address: Skalitzer str. 38
10999 Berlin Germany
Phone: +49 30 69533377

#134
Alois Oberbacher
Cuisines: Bavarian, Barbeque
Average price: €21-40
Area: Mitte
Address: Elisabethkirchstr. 2
10115 Berlin Germany
Phone: +49 30 47377305

#135
Sahara
Cuisines: African, Vegetarian
Average price: Under €7
Area: Neukölln
Address: Reuterstr. 56
12047 Berlin Germany
Phone: +49 30 47384090

#136
Pagode Thai Kitchen
Cuisines: Thai
Average price: €8-20
Area: Kreuzberg
Address: Bergmannstr. 88
10961 Berlin Germany
Phone: +49 30 6912640

#137
Fischfabrik
Cuisines: Fish & Chips
Average price: €8-20
Area: Prenzlauer Berg
Address: Danziger Str. 24
10435 Berlin Germany
Phone: +49 1515 2542387

#138
Chipps
Cuisines: European, Vegetarian
Average price: €8-20
Area: Mitte
Address: Jägerstr. 35
10117 Berlin Germany
Phone: +49 30 36444588

#139
Ohlala
Cuisines: Vegan
Average price: Under €7
Area: Friedrichshain
Address: Mainzerstr. 18
10247 Berlin Germany
Phone: +49 30 96086766

#140
Café Quitte
Cuisines: Cafe
Average price: Under €7
Area: Kreuzberg
Address: Wiener Str. 62
10999 Berlin Germany
Phone: +49 30 55147977

#141
Osmanya Restaurant
Cuisines: Turkish
Average price: €21-40
Area: Tiergarten
Address: Birkenstr. 17
10559 Berlin Germany
Phone: +49 30 48829997

#142
Gaststätte Heising
Cuisines: French
Average price: €21-40
Area: Wilmersdorf
Address: Rankestr. 32
10789 Berlin Germany
Phone: +49 30 2133952

#143
Salumeria Sigismondo
Cuisines: Cafe, Italian, Pizza
Average price: Under €7
Area: Prenzlauer Berg
Address: Kopenhagener Straße 6
10437 Berlin Germany
Phone: +49 30 81700132

#144
Azzam
Cuisines: Middle Eastern, Arabian
Average price: Under €7
Area: Neukölln
Address: Sonnenallee 54
12045 Berlin Germany
Phone: +49 30 30131541

#145
Restaurant Salento
Cuisines: Pizza, Italian
Average price: €8-20
Area: Wilmersdorf
Address: Eisenzahnstraße 16
10709 Berlin Germany
Phone: +49 30 89005600

#146
Marechiaro
Cuisines: Italian
Average price: €8-20
Area: Kreuzberg
Address: Wrangelstr.17
10997 Berlin Germany
Phone: +49 30 69568559

#147
Nil
Cuisines: African
Average price: Under €7
Area: Kreuzberg
Address: Oppelnerstr.4
10997 Berlin Germany
Phone: +49 30 48816414

#148
Le Compagnon
Cuisines: French
Average price: €21-40
Area: Wilmersdorf
Address: Knesebeckstr. 76
10623 Berlin Germany
Phone: +49 30 30347555

#149
Schleusenkrug
Cuisines: Barbeque
Average price: €8-20
Area: Tiergarten
Address: Müller-Breslau-Str. 1
10623 Berlin Germany
Phone: +49 30 3139909

#150
Schwarzer Hahn
Cuisines: German
Average price: €21-40
Area: Friedrichshain
Address: Seumestr. 23
10245 Berlin Germany
Phone: +49 30 21970371

#151
Papà Pane di Sorrento
Cuisines: Italian
Average price: €8-20
Area: Mitte
Address: Ackerstr. 23
10115 Berlin Germany
Phone: +49 30 28092701

#152
Rootz Berlin
Cuisines: Vegetarian, Cafe, Vegan
Average price: €8-20
Area: Kreuzberg
Address: Skalitzer Str. 75
10997 Berlin Germany
Phone: +49 1522 5839976

#153
Asaad
Cuisines: Middle Eastern,
Vegan, Arabian
Average price: €8-20
Area: Wedding
Address: Luxemburger Str.6
13353 Berlin Germany
Phone: +49 30 81799951

#154
Cantinetta Trattoria &Pizzaria
Cuisines: Italian
Average price: €8-20
Area: Charlottenburg
Address: Goethestr. 38
10625 Berlin Germany
Phone: +49 30 32667856

#155
Fräulein Fiona
Cuisines: German
Average price: €21-40
Area: Charlottenburg
Address: Fritschestr. 48
10627 Berlin Germany
Phone: +49 30 95602272

#156
Pepe Nero
Cuisines: Italian
Average price: €8-20
Area: Prenzlauer Berg
Address: Bötzowstr. 30
10407 Berlin Germany
Phone: +49 30 63968298

#157
Saigon New
Cuisines: Vietnamese
Average price: Under €7
Area: Prenzlauer Berg
Address: Prenzlauer Allee 196
10405 Berlin Germany
Phone: +49 30 78891331

#158
La Galleria Italiana
Cuisines: Italian
Average price: €8-20
Area: Mitte
Address: Torstr. 182
10115 Berlin Germany
Phone: +49 30 27572948

#159
Manngo Vietnam-Restaurant
Cuisines: Vietnamese
Average price: Under €7
Area: Mitte
Address: Mulackstr. 29
10119 Berlin Germany
Phone: +49 30 28040558

#160
Trattoria Perla Jonica
Cuisines: Italian
Average price: €8-20
Area: Schöneberg
Address: Belziger Str. 20
10823 Berlin Germany
Phone: +49 30 78710005

#161
Curcuma Restaurant-Bar
Cuisines: Japanese, Vietnamese
Average price: €8-20
Area: Mitte
Address: Karl-Marx-Allee 35
10178 Berlin Germany
Phone: +49 30 40042800

#162
Kulturhaus Insel Berlin
Cuisines: International
Average price: Under €7
Area: Treptow
Address: Alt-Treptow 6
12435 Berlin Germany
Phone: +49 30 80961850

#163
Nord - Sud
Cuisines: French
Average price: Under €7
Area: Mitte
Address: Auguststr. 87
10117 Berlin Germany
Phone: +49 30 97005928

#164
Segelschiffrestaurant Klipper
Cuisines: German
Average price: €8-20
Area: Treptow
Address: Bulgarische Str. 0
12435 Berlin Germany
Phone: +49 30 53216490

#165
Nini e Pettirosso
Cuisines: Pizza, Italian
Average price: Under €7
Area: Neukölln
Address: Selkestr. 27
12051 Berlin Germany
Phone: +49 30 68813061

#166
W Der Imbiss
Cuisines: Vegan, Fast Food
Average price: €8-20
Area: Mitte
Address: Kastanienallee 49
10119 Berlin Germany
Phone: +49 30 44352206

#167
A Magica
Cuisines: Italian, Pizza
Average price: €8-20
Area: Prenzlauer Berg
Address: Greifenhagener Str. 54
10437 Berlin Germany
Phone: +49 30 22808290

#168
Salumeria Culinario
Cuisines: Italian, Breakfast & Brunch
Average price: €8-20
Area: Mitte
Address: Tucholskystr. 34
10117 Berlin Germany
Phone: +49 30 28096767

#169
Café des Artistes
Cuisines: German, Mediterranean
Average price: €21-40
Area: Schöneberg
Address: Fuggerstr. 35
10777 Berlin Germany
Phone: +49 30 23635249

#170
Gugelhof
Cuisines: French, German
Average price: €21-40
Area: Prenzlauer Berg
Address: Kollwitzplatz
10435 Berlin Germany
Phone: +49 30 4429229

#171
Schlesisch Blau
Cuisines: French
Average price: €8-20
Area: Kreuzberg
Address: Köpenicker Str. 1a
10997 Berlin Germany
Phone: +49 30 69814538

#172
Chalet
Cuisines: German
Average price: €8-20
Area: Kreuzberg
Address: Vor dem Schlesischen Tor 3
10997 Berlin Germany
Phone: +49 30 69533766

#173
Kurhaus Korsakow
Cuisines: German, Breakfast & Brunch
Average price: €8-20
Area: Friedrichshain
Address: Grünbergerstr. 81
10245 Berlin Germany
Phone: +49 30 54737786

#174
Cassonade
Cuisines: Desserts, Creperies
Average price: €8-20
Area: Kreuzberg
Address: Oranienstr. 199
10999 Berlin Germany
Phone: +49 163 -1648559

#175
Curry Mitte
Cuisines: Curry Sausage
Average price: Under €7
Area: Mitte
Address: Torstr. 122
10119 Berlin Germany
Phone: +49 1520 1069559

#176
Hilde
Cuisines: Cafe
Average price: €8-20
Area: Prenzlauer Berg
Address: Metzerstr. 22
10405 Berlin Germany
Phone: +49 30 40504172

#177
Prater Garten
Cuisines: German
Average price: €8-20
Area: Prenzlauer Berg
Address: Kastanienallee 7-9
10435 Berlin Germany
Phone: +49 30 4485688

#178
Gaststätte Don Camillo
Cuisines: Italian
Average price: €21-40
Area: Charlottenburg
Address: Schloßstr. 7 14059
Berlin Germany
Phone: +49 30 3223572

#179
Mokalola
Cuisines: Cafe
Average price: €8-20
Area: Schöneberg
Address: Leberstr. 21
10829 Berlin Germany
Phone: +49 30 53166992

#180
Pizzaklub
Cuisines: Italian, Pizza
Average price: €8-20
Area: Schöneberg
Address: Katzlerstr. 10
10829 Berlin Germany
Phone: +49 30 23639400

#181
Taquería Ta'Cabrón Xberg
Cuisines: Mexican
Average price: Under €7
Area: Kreuzberg
Address: Skalitzer Str. 60
10997 Berlin Germany
Phone: +49 30 32662439

#182
Hugos
Cuisines: German, European
Average price: Above €41
Area: Tiergarten
Address: Budapester Str. 2
10787 Berlin Germany
Phone: +49 30 26021263

#183
Midtown Grill
Cuisines: Steakhouse, Barbeque,
Breakfast & Brunch, Barbeque
Average price: €21-40
Area: Tiergarten
Address: Ebertstr. 3
10117 Berlin Germany
Phone: +49 30 220006410

#184
Feines aus Österreich
Cuisines: Specialty Food, Austrian
Average price: Under €7
Area: Charlottenburg
Address: Leonhardtstr. 11
14057 Berlin Germany
Phone: +49 30 31016820

#185
Fräulein Burger
Cuisines: Burgers
Average price: €8-20
Area: Mitte
Address: Koppenplatz 1
10115 Berlin Germany
Phone: +49 30 46720908

#186
Ristorante I Due Emigranti
Cuisines: Italian
Average price: €21-40
Area: Schöneberg
Address: Belziger Str. 38
10823 Berlin Germany
Phone: +49 30 7826326

#187
Chi Chu
Cuisines: Vietnamese
Average price: €8-20
Area: Kreuzberg
Address: Lausitzer Platz 14
10997 Berlin Germany
Phone: +49 30 81803482

#188
Sarod's Thairestaurant
Cuisines: Thai, Asian Fusion, Chinese
Average price: €8-20
Area: Kreuzberg
Address: Friesenstr. 22
10965 Berlin Germany
Phone: +49 30 69507333

#189
Unser Feines Restaurant
Cuisines: German
Average price: €8-20
Area: Steglitz
Address: Ringstraße 49a
12205 Berlin Germany
Phone: +49 30 81058245

#190
Omoni
Cuisines: Sushi Bar, Korean
Average price: €8-20
Area: Prenzlauer Berg
Address: Kopenhagener Str. 14
10437 Berlin Germany
Phone: +49 30 23619244

#191
Renger-Patzsch
Cuisines: German, French
Average price: €21-40
Area: Schöneberg
Address: Wartburgstr. 54
10823 Berlin Germany
Phone: +49 30 7842059

#192
China Restaurant Tian-Fu
Cuisines: Chinese
Average price: €8-20
Area: Wilmersdorf
Address: Uhlandstr. 142
10719 Berlin Germany
Phone: +49 30 8613015

#193
Hamy Sophie
Cuisines: Asian Fusion, Vietnamese
Average price: Under €7
Area: Charlottenburg
Address: Wilmersdorfer Str. 41-42
10627 Berlin Germany
Phone: +49 30 31517599

#194
Hamy Café
Cuisines: Vietnamese
Average price: Under €7
Area: Kreuzberg
Address: Hasenheide 10
10967 Berlin Germany
Phone: +49 30 61625959

#195
Baraka
Cuisines: Moroccan, Lebanese
Average price: Under €7
Area: Kreuzberg
Address: Lausitzer Platz 6
10997 Berlin Germany
Phone: +49 30 6126330

#196
Weinschenke Weinstein
Cuisines: German, Coffee & Tea
Average price: €21-40
Area: Prenzlauer Berg
Address: Lychenerstr. 33
10437 Berlin Germany
Phone: +49 30 4411842

#197
Gaststätte Suppengrün
Cuisines: Soup
Average price: €8-20
Area: Mitte
Address: Inselstr. 1a
10179 Berlin Germany
Phone: +49 30 24781390

#198
G wie Goulasch
Cuisines: German
Average price: €8-20
Area: Kreuzberg
Address: Chamissoplatz 1
10965 Berlin Germany
Phone: +49 30 22439129

#199
Zum Schusterjungen
Cuisines: German
Average price: Under €7
Area: Prenzlauer Berg
Address: Danzigerstr. 9
10435 Berlin Germany
Phone: +49 30 4427654

#200
Knofi Café
Cuisines: Specialty Food, Coffee & Tea
Average price: €8-20
Area: Kreuzberg
Address: Bergmannstr. 11
10961 Berlin Germany
Phone: +49 30 69564359

#201
**RiCE UP Organic
Onigiri Kreuzberg**
Cuisines: Japanese
Average price: €8-20
Area: Kreuzberg
Address: Schönleinstr
10967 Berlin Germany
Phone: +49 30 81036617

#202
Lon-Men's Noodle House
Cuisines: Chinese, Taiwanese
Average price: Under €7
Area: Charlottenburg
Address: Kantstr. 33
10625 Berlin Germany
Phone: +49 30 31519678

#203
Muret La Barba
Cuisines: Italian, Wineries
Average price: €8-20
Area: Mitte
Address: Rosenthaler Str. 61
10119 Berlin Germany
Phone: +49 30 28097212

#204
Ron Telesky
Cuisines: Pizza
Average price: Under €7
Area: Kreuzberg
Address: Dieffenbachstr. 62
10967 Berlin Germany
Phone: +49 30 616211111

#205
Butterstulle Persicke
Cuisines: Bistro, Sandwiches
Average price: €8-20
Area: Mitte
Address: Marienstr. 25
10117 Berlin Germany
Phone: +49 30 28047532

#206
DaBangg
Cuisines: Korean
Average price: €8-20
Area: Schöneberg
Address: Hedwigstr. 18
12159 Berlin Germany
Phone: +49 30 95629407

#207
Margaux
Cuisines: French
Average price: Above €41
Area: Mitte
Address: Unter den Linden 78
10117 Berlin Germany
Phone: +49 30 22652611

#208
Grünfisch
Cuisines: Italian
Average price: €21-40
Area: Kreuzberg
Address: Graefestr. 26a
10967 Berlin Germany
Phone: +49 30 61621252

#209
Minh-Trang
Cuisines: Vietnamese
Average price: Under €7
Area: Charlottenburg
Address: Kantstr. 67
10627 Berlin Germany
Phone: +49 30 31801117

#210
Die Feinbäckerei
Cuisines: Swabian, German
Average price: €8-20
Area: Schöneberg
Address: Vorbergstr. 2
10823 Berlin Germany
Phone: +49 30 81494240

#211
Big Stuff Smoked BBQ
Cuisines: American, Fast Food
Average price: €8-20
Area: Kreuzberg
Address: Eisenbahnstr. 42/43
10997 Berlin Germany
Phone: +49 163 6290413

#212
MarienBurger
Cuisines: Burgers
Average price: Under €7
Area: Prenzlauer Berg
Address: Marienburger Str. 47
10405 Berlin Germany
Phone: +49 30 30340515

#213
Dirty South
Cuisines: Mexican
Average price: €8-20
Area: Friedrichshain
Address: Krossenerstr. 18
10245 Berlin Germany
Phone: +49 30 29360555

#214
Aigner Gendarmenmarkt
Cuisines: German, Austrian
Average price: €21-40
Area: Mitte
Address: Französischestr. 25
10117 Berlin Germany
Phone: +49 30 203751850

#215
Volver
Cuisines: Tapas
Average price: €8-20
Area: Mitte
Address: Luisenstr. 41
10117 Berlin Germany
Phone: +49 30 27572164

#216
AmmAmma
Cuisines: Indian
Average price: Under €7
Area: Schöneberg
Address: Eisenacher Straße 59
10823 Berlin Germany
Phone: +49 30 78718485

#217
Rice Queen
Cuisines: Chinese, Indonesian,
Asian Fusion
Average price: Under €7
Area: Prenzlauer Berg
Address: Danziger Str. 13
10435 Berlin Germany
Phone: +49 30 44045800

#218
Thai-Bistro Jasmin
Cuisines: Vietnamese, Thai
Average price: Under €7
Area: Neukölln
Address: Hermannstr. 45
12049 Berlin Germany
Phone: +49 30 6271680

#219
Ess Werk Berlin
Cuisines: German, Swabian
Average price: Under €7
Area: Schöneberg
Address: Nollendorfstr. 21a
10777 Berlin Germany
Phone: +49 30 21919757

#220
Esszimmer
Cuisines: German
Average price: €21-40
Area: Mitte
Address: Scharnhorststr. 28-29
10115 Berlin Germany
Phone: +49 30 2021530-1

#221
Onkel Ho
Cuisines: Vietnamese, Asian Fusion
Average price: €8-20
Area: Prenzlauer Berg
Address: Gleimstr. 11
10437 Berlin Germany
Phone: +49 30 44356379

#222
Smart Deli
Cuisines: Japanese
Average price: €8-20
Area: Mitte
Address: Chausseestr.5
10115 Berlin Germany
Phone: +49 30 20687037

#223
Amici Amici
Cuisines: Italian, Cafe, Pizza
Average price: €8-20
Area: Kreuzberg
Address: Mehringdamm 40
10961 Berlin Germany
Phone: +49 30 7468412

#224
Frühsammers Restaurant
Cuisines: German
Average price: €21-40
Area: Wilmersdorf
Address: Flinsberger Platz 8 14193
Berlin Germany
Phone: +49 30 89738628

#225
Spreegold
Cuisines: Breakfast & Brunch
Average price: €8-20
Area: Prenzlauer Berg
Address: Hufelandstr. 20
10407 Berlin Germany
Phone: +49 30 41935081

#226
Goûter
Cuisines: German, French
Average price: Under €7
Area: Kreuzberg
Address: Reichenbergerstr. 143
10999 Berlin Germany
Phone: +49 30 35125162

#227
Taverna Cassambalis
Cuisines: Greek
Average price: €21-40
Area: Wilmersdorf
Address: Grolmanstr. 35
10623 Berlin Germany
Phone: +49 30 8854747

#228
Zuckerstück
Cuisines: Cafe
Average price: €8-20
Area: Prenzlauer Berg
Address: Schivelbeinerstr. 7
10439 Berlin Germany
Phone: +49 160 92891269

#229
Spätzle Express
Cuisines: German, Vegetarian, Swabian
Average price: €8-20
Area: Kreuzberg
Address: Wienerstr. 11
10999 Berlin Germany
Phone: +49 30 69534463

#230
Vaust
Cuisines: Vegetarian, Vegan
Average price: €8-20
Area: Charlottenburg
Address: Pestalozzistr. 8
10625 Berlin Germany
Phone: +49 30 54599160

#231
Engelbecken
Cuisines: German, Austrian
Average price: €21-40
Area: Charlottenburg
Address: Witzlebenstr. 31
14057 Berlin Germany
Phone: +49 30 6152810

#232
YamYam
Cuisines: Korean
Average price: €8-20
Area: Mitte
Address: Alte Schönhauser Str 6
10119 Berlin Germany
Phone: +49 30 24632485

#233
CapeTown Berlin
Cuisines: African, Lounge
Average price: €21-40
Area: Prenzlauer Berg
Address: Schönfließer Str. 15
10439 Berlin Germany
Phone: +49 30 40057658

#234
Pure Origins
Cuisines: Cafe
Average price: Under €7
Area: Mitte
Address: Georgenstr. 193
10117 Berlin Germany
Phone: +49 177 2930098

#235
Five Elephant
Cuisines: Bakeries, Cafe
Average price: €8-20
Area: Kreuzberg
Address: Reichenbergerstr. 101
10999 Berlin Germany
Phone: +49 30 96081527

#236
Sachiko Sushi
Cuisines: Sushi Bar
Average price: €21-40
Area: Charlottenburg
Address: Jeanne-Mammen-Bogen 584
10623 Berlin Germany
Phone: +49 30 3132282

#237
El-Rief
Cuisines: Middle Eastern, Kebab
Average price: Under €7
Area: Prenzlauer Berg
Address: Schönhauser Allee 47
10437 Berlin Germany
Phone: +49 30 69523888

#238
Schwarzwaldstuben
Cuisines: German, Breakfast & Brunch
Average price: €8-20
Area: Mitte
Address: Tucholskystr. 48
10117 Berlin Germany
Phone: +49 30 28098084

#239
Wirtshaus Zum Mitterhofer
Cuisines: German
Average price: €8-20
Area: Kreuzberg
Address: Fichtestr. 33
10967 Berlin Germany
Phone: +49 30 34711008

#240
Schneeweiß-Berlin
Cuisines: German, European
Average price: €21-40
Area: Friedrichshain
Address: Simplonstr. 16
10245 Berlin Germany
Phone: +49 30 29049704

#241
To Loc
Cuisines: Vietnamese,
Vegetarian, Korean
Average price: Under €7
Area: Kreuzberg
Address: Wiener Str. 61
10999 Berlin Germany
Phone: +49 30 32505346

#242
Gaststätte Dwin
Cuisines: German
Average price: €21-40
Area: Wilmersdorf
Address: Uhlandstr. 157
10719 Berlin Germany
Phone: +49 30 8812915

#243
Café Einstein
Cuisines: Cafe
Average price: €21-40
Area: Tiergarten
Address: Kurfürstenstr. 58
10785 Berlin Germany
Phone: +49 30 2615096

#244
La Cocotte
Cuisines: French, Wine Bar
Average price: €8-20
Area: Schöneberg
Address: Vorbergstr. 10
10823 Berlin Germany
Phone: +49 30 78957658

#245
Maroush
Cuisines: Middle Eastern
Average price: Under €7
Area: Kreuzberg
Address: Adalbertstr. 93
10999 Berlin Germany
Phone: +49 30 69536171

#246
Burgers Berlin
Cuisines: Burgers, Fast Food
Average price: €8-20
Area: Friedrichshain
Address: Sonntagstr. 2
10245 Berlin Germany
Phone: +49 30 29364069

#247
Jules Verne
Cuisines: French
Average price: €8-20
Area: Charlottenburg
Address: Schlüterstr. 61
10625 Berlin Germany
Phone: +49 30 31809410

#248
Syrtaki
Cuisines: Greek
Average price: €8-20
Area: Weißensee
Address: Alt-Blankenburg 22
13129 Berlin Germany
Phone: +49 30 47485977

#249
Asado Steakhaus
Cuisines: Argentine, Steakhouse
Average price: €8-20
Area: Reinickendorf
Address: Scharnweberstr. 67
13405 Berlin Germany
Phone: +49 30 4138313

#250
Al-Faruk
Cuisines: Oriental
Average price: Under €7
Area: Kreuzberg
Address: Wrangelstr. 46
10997 Berlin Germany
Phone: +49 179 9464580

#251
Henne
Cuisines: German
Average price: €8-20
Area: Kreuzberg
Address: Leuschnerdamm 25
10999 Berlin Germany
Phone: +49 30 6147730

#252
Boccondivino
Cuisines: Italian
Average price: €8-20
Area: Mitte
Address: Albrechtstr. 18
10117 Berlin Germany
Phone: +49 30 28493898

#253
Minh Quang
Cuisines: Thai, Vietnamese
Average price: Under €7
Area: Prenzlauer Berg
Address: Greifswalder Str. 216
10405 Berlin Germany
Phone: +49 30 44352062

#254
Café Jule
Cuisines: Cafe
Average price: Under €7
Area: Neukölln
Address: Kienitzer Str. 93
12049 Berlin Germany
Phone: +49 30 74695980

#255
Makoto
Cuisines: Japanese, Soup
Average price: €8-20
Area: Mitte
Address: Alte Schönhauserstr. 13
10119 Berlin Germany
Phone: +49 30 97893857

#256
Ming Dynastie
Cuisines: Chinese, Asian Fusion
Average price: €8-20
Area: Mitte
Address: Brückenstr. 6
10179 Berlin Germany
Phone: +49 30 30875680

#257
Indian Dhaba Mira
Cuisines: Indian
Average price: Under €7
Area: Neukölln
Address: Pannierstr. 40
12047 Berlin Germany
Phone: +49 30 62901532

#258
Koy
Cuisines: Thai
Average price: Under €7
Area: Friedrichshain
Address: Rigaerstr. 26
10247 Berlin Germany
Phone: +49 30 40043988

#259
Dicke Wirtin
Cuisines: German
Average price: €8-20
Area: Charlottenburg
Address: Carmerstr. 9
10623 Berlin Germany
Phone: +49 30 3124952

#260
Tadshikische Teestube
Cuisines: Asian Fusion, Russian
Average price: €8-20
Area: Mitte
Address: Oranienburger Str. 27
10117 Berlin Germany
Phone: +49 30 2041112

#261
Samos, Griechisches Restaurant
Cuisines: Greek
Average price: €8-20
Area: Wilmersdorf
Address: Leibnizstr. 56
10629 Berlin Germany
Phone: +49 30 8836111

#262
Ixthys
Cuisines: Korean
Average price: €8-20
Area: Schöneberg
Address: Pallasstr. 21
10781 Berlin Germany
Phone: +49 30 81474769

#263
Café im Zeughaus
Cuisines: Cafe
Average price: €21-40
Area: Mitte
Address: Unter den Linden 2
10117 Berlin Germany
Phone: +49 30 20642744

#264
Sushi TTP & More
Cuisines: Sushi Bar, Japanese
Average price: Under €7
Area: Wilmersdorf
Address: Olivaer Platz 6
10707 Berlin Germany
Phone: +49 30 88709887

#265
Fräulein Dickes
Cuisines: Coffee & Tea,
Breakfast & Brunch
Average price: €8-20
Area: Prenzlauer Berg
Address: Stargarder Str. 60
10437 Berlin Germany
Phone: +49 30 77904900

#266
Tapitas
Cuisines: Cafe, Tapas Bar
Average price: €8-20
Area: Prenzlauer Berg
Address: Gleimstr. 23
10437 Berlin Germany
Phone: +49 30 46736837

#267
Pamfilya
Cuisines: Turkish, Kebab
Average price: €8-20
Area: Wedding
Address: Luxemburger Str. 1
13353 Berlin Germany
Phone: +49 30 4532699

#268
Jin Dal Le
Cuisines: Korean
Average price: €8-20
Area: Wedding
Address: Fennstr. 4
13347 Berlin Germany
Phone: +49 30 4656527

#269
Shochu Bar
Cuisines: Bar, Japanese
Average price: €21-40
Area: Mitte
Address: Behrenstr. 72
10117 Berlin Germany
Phone: +49 30 301117328

#270
Colibri
Cuisines: Mediterranean, Tapas
Average price: €8-20
Area: Kreuzberg
Address: Chamissoplatz 1
10965 Berlin Germany
Phone: +49 177 3006813

#271
Ristorante a Mano
Cuisines: Italian
Average price: €8-20
Area: Mitte
Address: Strausberger Platz 2
10243 Berlin Germany
Phone: +49 30 95598243

#272
Mamecha
Cuisines: Japanese
Average price: €8-20
Area: Mitte
Address: Mulackstr. 33
10119 Berlin Germany
Phone: +49 30 28884264

#273
Joseph-Roth-Diele
Cuisines: German
Average price: Under €7
Area: Tiergarten
Address: Potsdamer Str. 75
10785 Berlin Germany
Phone: +49 30 26369884

#274
Zwiebelfisch Gaststätten
Cuisines: German
Average price: €8-20
Area: Charlottenburg
Address: Savignyplatz 7
10623 Berlin Germany
Phone: +49 30 3127363

#275
Osteria Ribaltone
Cuisines: Italian
Average price: €8-20
Area: Schöneberg
Address: Motzstr. 54
10777 Berlin Germany
Phone: +49 30 2143655

#276
DasWins
Cuisines: German, International
Average price: €8-20
Area: Prenzlauer Berg
Address: Winsstr. 53
10405 Berlin Germany
Phone: +49 30 31165572

#277
Restaurant Nemesis
Cuisines: Greek
Average price: €8-20
Area: Schöneberg
Address: Hauptstr. 154
10827 Berlin Germany
Phone: +49 30 7811590

#278
Zio Felix
Cuisines: Pizza
Average price: €8-20
Area: Neukölln
Address: Okerstr. 35
12049 Berlin Germany
Phone: +49 176 59948695

#279
Santa Maria
Cuisines: Mexican
Average price: €8-20
Area: Kreuzberg
Address: Oranienstr. 170
10999 Berlin Germany
Phone: +49 30 92210027

#280
Yumcha Heroes
Cuisines: Chinese
Average price: €8-20
Area: Mitte
Address: Weinbergsweg 8
10119 Berlin Germany
Phone: +49 30 76213035

#281
Regenbogenfabrik
Cuisines: German
Average price: Under €7
Area: Kreuzberg
Address: Lausitzer Str. 22
10999 Berlin Germany
Phone: +49 30 6957950

#282
Varadero
Cuisines: Cuban, Cocktail Bar
Average price: €8-20
Area: Schöneberg
Address: Vorbergstraße 11
10823 Berlin Germany
Phone: +49 30 78716667

#283
Mr. Vertigo
Cuisines: Sandwiches
Average price: Under €7
Area: Mitte
Address: Chausseestr. 17
10115 Berlin Germany
Phone: +49 163 6010110

#284
Kabir
Cuisines: Indian
Average price: €8-20
Area: Charlottenburg
Address: Carmerstr. 17
10623 Berlin Germany
Phone: +49 30 3128157

#285
Carabao
Cuisines: Bar, Thai
Average price: €8-20
Area: Kreuzberg
Address: Hornstraße 4
10963 Berlin Germany
Phone: +49 30 21753082

#286
Coffee Break
Cuisines: Cafe
Average price: Under €7
Area: Tiergarten
Address: Jagowstraße 23
10555 Berlin Germany
Phone: +49 30 89392767

#287
Jolesch
Cuisines: European, Austrian
Average price: €21-40
Area: Kreuzberg
Address: Muskauer Str. 1
10997 Berlin Germany
Phone: +49 30 6123581

#288
Masaniello
Cuisines: Italian
Average price: €8-20
Area: Kreuzberg
Address: Hasenheide 20
10967 Berlin Germany
Phone: +49 30 6926657

#289
Nil
Cuisines: Vegetarian, African
Average price: Under €7
Area: Friedrichshain
Address: Grünberger Str. 52
10245 Berlin Germany
Phone: +49 30 29047713

#290
Romantica
Cuisines: Pub, Italian
Average price: €8-20
Area: Schöneberg
Address: Akazienstr. 7A
10823 Berlin Germany
Phone: +49 30 7845518

#291
Gözleme Restaurant
Cuisines: Turkish
Average price: Under €7
Area: Neukölln
Address: Karl-Marx-Str. 35
12043 Berlin Germany
Phone: +49 30 6134134

#292
Trattoria Felice
Cuisines: European
Average price: €8-20
Area: Prenzlauer Berg
Address: Lychener Str. 41
10437 Berlin Germany
Phone: +49 30 40041927

#293
Casa Matti
Cuisines: Italian
Average price: €21-40
Area: Tiergarten
Address: Helgoländer Ufer 7
10557 Berlin Germany
Phone: +49 30 98331150

#294
Café Seeblick
Cuisines: Cafe, German
Average price: €8-20
Area: Prenzlauer Berg
Address: Rykestr. 14
10405 Berlin Germany
Phone: +49 30 4429226

#295
Carlo & Rita Pizza Pasta Vino
Cuisines: Pizza, Italian
Average price: €8-20
Area: Reinickendorf
Address: Schubartstr. 47
13509 Berlin Germany
Phone: +49 30 4328015

#296
Neumond Kaffeehaus
& Restaurant
Cuisines: German, Breakfast & Brunch
Average price: €8-20
Area: Mitte
Address: Borsigstr. 28
10115 Berlin Germany
Phone: +49 30 2857505

#297
Khushi
Cuisines: Indian, Coffee & Tea
Average price: Under €7
Area: Prenzlauer Berg
Address: Kollwitzstr. 37
10405 Berlin Germany
Phone: +49 30 48493791

#298
Arlecchino - Ristorante Italiano
Cuisines: Italian
Average price: €21-40
Area: Wilmersdorf
Address: Meinekestr. 25
10719 Berlin Germany
Phone: +49 30 8812563

#299
Locanda
Cuisines: Italian
Average price: Under €7
Area: Wilmersdorf
Address: Lehniner Platz 2
10709 Berlin Germany
Phone: +49 30 31806968

#300
Angkor Wat
Cuisines: Cambodian, Vietnamese
Average price: €8-20
Area: Tiergarten
Address: Paulstr. 22
10557 Berlin Germany
Phone: +49 30 3933922

#301
Rickenbackers Music Inn
Cuisines: International
Average price: €8-20
Area: Wilmersdorf
Address: Bundesallee 194b
10717 Berlin Germany
Phone: +49 30 81898290

#302
Cafè Marcello
Cuisines: Italian
Average price: €8-20
Area: Schöneberg
Address: Fritz-Reuter-Str. 7
10827 Berlin Germany
Phone: +49 30 81828584

#303
La Piadina
Cuisines: Fast Food, Bistro
Average price: Under €7
Area: Charlottenburg
Address: Leonhardtstr. 7
14057 Berlin Germany
Phone: +49 30 68073637

#304
Thai Inside
Cuisines: Thai, Bar, Asian Fusion
Average price: €8-20
Area: Mitte
Address: Dircksenstr. 37
10178 Berlin Germany
Phone: +49 30 24724371

#305
Thai-Elephant
Cuisines: Thai
Average price: €8-20
Area: Wilmersdorf
Address: Fasanenstraße 15
10623 Berlin Germany
Phone: +49 30 88624853

#306
Maria Café & Restaurant
Cuisines: German, Italian
Average price: €8-20
Area: Wilmersdorf
Address: Bundesallee 181
10717 Berlin Germany
Phone: +49 30 85406905

#307
Maru
Cuisines: Korean
Average price: €8-20
Area: Friedrichshain
Address: Rigaer Str. 74
10247 Berlin Germany
Phone: +49 30 26545652

#308
Il Tinello
Cuisines: Italian, Pizza
Average price: €8-20
Area: Friedrichshain
Address: Samariterstr. 28
10247 Berlin Germany
Phone: +49 30 29048232

#309
Falafel Daye
Cuisines: Middle Eastern, Kebab
Average price: Under €7
Area: Prenzlauer Berg
Address: Danziger Str. 24
10435 Berlin Germany
Phone: +49 30 44046373

#310
Mutzenbacher
Cuisines: Austrian
Average price: €8-20
Area: Friedrichshain
Address: Libauerstr. 11
10245 Berlin Germany
Phone: +49 30 95616788

#311
Zaika
Cuisines: Indian
Average price: €8-20
Area: Prenzlauer Berg
Address: Wichertstr. 57
10439 Berlin Germany
Phone: +49 30 40003435

#312
SnackTime
Cuisines: Soup
Average price: €8-20
Area: Tempelhof
Address: Mariendorfer Damm 77
12109 Berlin Germany
Phone: +49 30 76766078

#313
Gaststätte La Cantina
Cuisines: Italian
Average price: €21-40
Area: Wilmersdorf
Address: Bleibtreustr. 17
10623 Berlin Germany
Phone: +49 30 8832156

#314
Mädchen ohne Abitur
Cuisines: German, Mediterranean
Average price: €8-20
Area: Kreuzberg
Address: Körtestr. 5
10967 Berlin Germany
Phone: +49 30 61625860

#315
Cotto e Crudo
Cuisines: Italian
Average price: €8-20
Area: Prenzlauer Berg
Address: Eberswalderstr.33
10437 Berlin Germany
Phone: +49 30 44037111

#316
Oktogon Fusion
Cuisines: Restaurants
Average price: €21-40
Area: Mitte
Address: Leipziger Platz 10
10117 Berlin Germany
Phone: +49 30 20642864

#317
Chefétage
Cuisines: German, Mediterranean
Average price: €8-20
Area: Mitte
Address: Inselstr. 8
10179 Berlin Germany
Phone: +49 30 24723655

#318
Robbengatter
Cuisines: German, Mediterranean
Average price: €8-20
Area: Schöneberg
Address: Grunewaldstr. 55
10825 Berlin Germany
Phone: +49 30 8535255

#319
Bandol Sur Mer
Cuisines: French
Average price: €21-40
Area: Mitte
Address: Torstr. 167
10115 Berlin Germany
Phone: +49 30 67302051

#320
Lychee
Cuisines: Chinese
Average price: €8-20
Area: Wilmersdorf
Address: Bayerische Str 9
10707 Berlin Germany
Phone: +49 30 31179218

#321
Van Hoa
Cuisines: Vietnamese
Average price: Under €7
Area: Prenzlauer Berg
Address: Stargarder Str. 79
10437 Berlin Germany
Phone: +49 30 40574197

#322
Max & Moritz
Cuisines: German
Average price: €8-20
Area: Kreuzberg
Address: Oranienstr. 162
10969 Berlin Germany
Phone: +49 30 69515911

#323
De Molen
Cuisines: Fast Food
Average price: Under €7
Area: Friedrichshain
Address: Neue Bahnhofstr. 26a
10245 Berlin Germany
Phone: +49 30 81616710

#324
Udagawa
Cuisines: Japanese, Sushi Bar
Average price: €8-20
Area: Steglitz
Address: Feuerbachstr. 24
12163 Berlin Germany
Phone: +49 30 7922373

#325
Manzini
Cuisines: European, German
Average price: €8-20
Area: Wilmersdorf
Address: Ludwigkirchstr. 11
10719 Berlin Germany
Phone: +49 30 8857820

#326
Cafe Tomsky
Cuisines: Cafe
Average price: €8-20
Area: Prenzlauer Berg
Address: Winsstr. 61
10405 Berlin Germany
Phone: +49 30 4415922

#327
BR101
Cuisines: Brazilian
Average price: Under €7
Area: Prenzlauer Berg
Address: Torstr. 69
10119 Berlin Germany
Phone: +49 176 78409497

#328
Mr. Long & Friends
Cuisines: Vietnamese
Average price: €8-20
Area: Prenzlauer Berg
Address: Kollwitzstr. 87
10435 Berlin Germany
Phone: +49 30 44308493

#329
Gusto Giusto
Cuisines: Pizza
Average price: €8-20
Area: Charlottenburg
Address: Kaiserdamm 110
14057 Berlin Germany
Phone: +49 30 30109173

#330
Butter
Cuisines: Breakfast & Brunch
Average price: €8-20
Area: Prenzlauer Berg
Address: Pappelallee 73
10437 Berlin Germany
Phone: +49 30 52685933

#331
Sauvage
Cuisines: Gluten-Free, Specialty Food
Average price: €21-40
Area: Neukölln
Address: Pflügerstr. 25
12047 Berlin Germany
Phone: +49 30 53167547

#332
Devil's Kitchen & Bar
Cuisines: Mediterranean
Average price: €8-20
Area: Kreuzberg
Address: Graefestr. 11
10967 Berlin Germany
Phone: +49 176 60945942

#333
Restaurant Café Heideröschen
Cuisines: German, Mediterranean
Average price: €21-40
Area: Pankow
Address: Waldsteg 65
13158 Berlin Germany
Phone: +49 30 9167852

#334
Mädchenitaliener
Cuisines: Italian
Average price: €8-20
Area: Mitte
Address: Alte Schönhauser Str. 12
10119 Berlin Germany
Phone: +49 30 40041787

#335
Naveen Path
Cuisines: Indian
Average price: Under €7
Area: Wedding
Address: Tegeler Str. 21-22
13353 Berlin Germany
Phone: +49 30 45029460

#336
Quchnia
Cuisines: Cafe, Sandwiches
Average price: €8-20
Area: Mitte
Address: Markgrafenstr. 35
10117 Berlin Germany
Phone: +49 30 20609286

#337
3 Schwestern
Cuisines: Breakfast & Brunch
Average price: €21-40
Area: Kreuzberg
Address: Mariannenplatz 2
10997 Berlin Germany
Phone: +49 30 600318600

#338
Pavillon
Cuisines: European
Average price: €8-20
Area: Friedrichshain
Address: Friedenstr. 101
10249 Berlin Germany
Phone: +49 30 42080990

#339
Block House
Cuisines: Steakhouse
Average price: €21-40
Area: Mitte
Address: Karl-Liebknechtstr. 7
10178 Berlin Germany
Phone: +49 30 2423300

#340
Mammam Garküche
Cuisines: Vietnamese, Thai
Average price: Under €7
Area: Friedrichshain
Address: Gabriel Max Str. 2
10245 Berlin Germany
Phone: +49 30 20318482

#341
Ristorante Mario
Cuisines: Italian
Average price: €21-40
Area: Schöneberg
Address: Südwestkorso 10
12161 Berlin Germany
Phone: +49 30 83223915

#342
Mamay - Vietnamesisches Teehaus
Cuisines: Vietnamese, Chinese
Average price: €8-20
Area: Prenzlauer Berg
Address: Schönhauser Allee 61
10437 Berlin Germany
Phone: +49 30 4447270

#343
Good Time
Cuisines: Indonesian, Thai, Asian Fusion
Average price: €21-40
Area: Mitte
Address: Hausvogteiplatz 11
10117 Berlin Germany
Phone: +49 30 20074870

#344
Restaurant Tim Raue
Cuisines: Asian Fusion, European
Average price: Above €41
Area: Kreuzberg
Address: Rudi-Dutschke-Str. 26
10969 Berlin Germany
Phone: +49 30 25937930

#345
Nolas am Weinberg
Cuisines: European
Average price: €8-20
Area: Mitte
Address: Veteranenstr. 9
10119 Berlin Germany
Phone: +49 30 44040766

#346
Sigiriya
Cuisines: Asian Fusion
Average price: €8-20
Area: Friedrichshain
Address: Grünbergerstr. 66
10245 Berlin Germany
Phone: +49 30 29044208

#347
Masala
Cuisines: Indian
Average price: €8-20
Area: Charlottenburg
Address: Friedbergstr. 38
14057 Berlin Germany
Phone: +49 30 48481787

#348
Dos Palillos
Cuisines: Asian Fusion
Average price: €21-40
Area: Mitte
Address: Weinmeisterstr. 1
10178 Berlin Germany
Phone: +49 30 20003413

#349
Lokal
Cuisines: German
Average price: €21-40
Area: Mitte
Address: Linienstr. 160
10115 Berlin Germany
Phone: +49 30 28449500

#350
Das Meisterstück
Cuisines: German, Herbs & Spices
Average price: €21-40
Area: Mitte
Address: Hausvogteiplatz 3-4
10117 Berlin Germany
Phone: +49 30 55872562

#351
Kasbah
Cuisines: Moroccan
Average price: €8-20
Area: Mitte
Address: Gipsstr. 2
10119 Berlin Germany
Phone: +49 30 27594361

#352
Die Garbe
Cuisines: European,
Food Delivery Services
Average price: Under €7
Area: Friedrichshain
Address: Frankfurter Allee 40
10247 Berlin Germany
Phone: +49 30 29385204

#353
Restaurant Rems
Cuisines: Swabian
Average price: Under €7
Area: Steglitz
Address: Schildhornstr. 98
12163 Berlin Germany
Phone: +49 30 81820636

#354
Tempo-Box
Cuisines: International,
Breakfast & Brunch
Average price: €8-20
Area: Friedrichshain
Address: Simon-Dach-Str. 15
10245 Berlin Germany
Phone: +49 30 74078861

#355
Chicago Williams Bbq
Cuisines: Burgers
Average price: €8-20
Area: Mitte
Address: Hannoversche Str. 2
10115 Berlin Germany
Phone: +49 30 28042422

#356
Oliobiscotti
Cuisines: Italian, Wine Bar
Average price: Above €41
Area: Kreuzberg
Address: Graefestr. 39
10967 Berlin Germany
Phone: +49 30 66303434

#357
Lieu in Berlin
Cuisines: Vietnamese
Average price: €8-20
Area: Tiergarten
Address: Kurfürstenstr.112
10787 Berlin Germany
Phone: +49 30 93957474

#358
Solar
Cuisines: Bar, German, International
Average price: €21-40
Area: Kreuzberg
Address: Stesemannstr.76
10963 Berlin Germany
Phone: +49 163 7652700

#359
Roter Jäger
Cuisines: German
Average price: €21-40
Area: Mitte
Address: Jägerstr. 28-32
10117 Berlin Germany
Phone: +49 30 23257955

#360
Rotisserie Weingrün
Cuisines: Barbeque, German
Average price: €21-40
Area: Mitte
Address: Gertraudenstr. 10-12
10178 Berlin Germany
Phone: +44 30 2062 1900

#361
La Muse Gueule
Cuisines: French
Average price: €8-20
Area: Prenzlauer Berg
Address: Sredzkistr. 14
10435 Berlin Germany
Phone: +49 30 43206596

#362
Joris
Cuisines: Salad, Soup
Average price: Under €7
Area: Mitte
Address: Brunnenstr 158
10115 Berlin Germany
Phone: +49 4930 47365973

#363
Pho Phan
Cuisines: Vietnamese
Average price: Under €7
Area: Neukölln
Address: Hermannstr. 152
12051 Berlin Germany
Phone: +49 30 6290094647

#364
Raststätte Gnadenbrot
Cuisines: German
Average price: Under €7
Area: Schöneberg
Address: Martin-Luther-Str. 20A
10777 Berlin Germany
Phone: +49 30 21961786

#365
Volta
Cuisines: Burgers, American,
Asian Fusion
Average price: €8-20
Area: Wedding
Address: Brunnenstr. 73
13355 Berlin Germany
Phone: +49 178 3965490

#366
Mein Haus am See
Cuisines: Cafe, German
Average price: €8-20
Area: Mitte
Address: Brunnenstr. 197-198
10119 Berlin Germany
Phone: +49 30 23883561

#367
Café Dritter Raum
Cuisines: Cafe
Average price: Under €7
Area: Neukölln
Address: Hertzbergstr. 14
12055 Berlin Germany
Phone: +49 30 54737666

#368
Viet Village
Cuisines: Vietnamese
Average price: Under €7
Area: Mitte
Address: Rosenthalerstr. 50
10178 Berlin Germany
Phone: +49 30 24726477

#369
Nußbaumerin
Cuisines: Austrian, German
Average price: €8-20
Area: Wilmersdorf
Address: Leibnizstr. 55
10629 Berlin Germany
Phone: +49 30 50178033

#370
Märchenwaffel
Cuisines: Cafe
Average price: Under €7
Area: Friedrichshain
Address: Warschauer Str. 61
10243 Berlin Germany
Phone: +49 172 3196677

#371
Ishin
Cuisines: Japanese
Average price: €8-20
Area: Wilmersdorf
Address: Bundesallee 203
10717 Berlin Germany
Phone: +49 30 21016009

#372
Keule Berliner Mundart
Cuisines: German
Average price: €8-20
Area: Friedrichshain
Address: Simon Dach Str. 22
10245 Berlin Germany
Phone: +49 30 22345501

#373
Hasir
Cuisines: Turkish, Kebab, Fast Food
Average price: €21-40
Area: Mitte
Address: Oranienburger Str. 4
10178 Berlin Germany
Phone: +49 30 28041616

#374
Ishin
Cuisines: Sushi Bar, Japanese
Average price: €8-20
Area: Mitte
Address: Charlottenstr. 16
10117 Berlin Germany
Phone: +49 30 60500172

#375
Trattoria Peretti
Cuisines: Italian
Average price: €8-20
Area: Mitte
Address: Karl-Liebknecht-Str. 5
10178 Berlin Germany
Phone: +49 30 27908580

#376
Brauereigaststätte Leibhaftig
Cuisines: German, Breweries
Average price: €8-20
Area: Prenzlauer Berg
Address: Metzer Str. 30
10405 Berlin Germany
Phone: +49 30 54815039

#377
Blaue Tische
Cuisines: Vegetarian, Greek
Average price: €8-20
Area: Neukölln
Address: Friedelstr. 56
12047 Berlin Germany
Phone: +49 178 5101776

#378
Restaurant Z
Cuisines: Greek
Average price: €8-20
Area: Kreuzberg
Address: Friesenstr. 12
10965 Berlin Germany
Phone: +49 30 6922716

#379
Mamsellchen
Cuisines: Cafe
Average price: €8-20
Area: Tiergarten
Address: Elberfelder Str. 9
10555 Berlin Germany
Phone: +49 30 70088851

#380
Neugrüns Köche
Cuisines: European
Average price: €21-40
Area: Prenzlauer Berg
Address: Schönhauser Allee 135a
10437 Berlin Germany
Phone: +49 30 44012092

#381
Schiller Burger
Cuisines: Burgers, Bar
Average price: €8-20
Area: Neukölln
Address: Herrfurthstr. 7
12049 Berlin Germany
Phone: +49 172 9824427

#382
Le Provencal
Cuisines: French, Wine Bar
Average price: €21-40
Area: Mitte
Address: Spreeufer 3
10178 Berlin Germany
Phone: +49 30 3027567

#383
Zitrone
Cuisines: Mediterranean, Latin American,
Asian Fusion
Average price: €8-20
Area: Kreuzberg
Address: Graefestr. 20
10967 Berlin Germany
Phone: +49 30 61626556

#384
Spreestern Restaurant
Cuisines: German
Average price: €21-40
Area: Kreuzberg
Address: Köpenicker Str. 174
10997 Berlin Germany
Phone: +49 30 50566369

#385
Restaurant Zander
Cuisines: German
Average price: €21-40
Area: Prenzlauer Berg
Address: Kollwitzstr. 50
10405 Berlin Germany
Phone: +49 30 44057678

#386
Stadtklause
Cuisines: German
Average price: Under €7
Area: Kreuzberg
Address: Bernburger Str. 35
10963 Berlin Germany
Phone: +49 30 51056381

#387
Auf Die Hand
Cuisines: Fast Food, Desserts, Salad
Average price: €8-20
Area: Mitte
Address: Luisenstr. 45
10117 Berlin Germany
Phone: +49 30 48823759

#388
Vineria del Este
Cuisines: Spanish, Tapas Bar
Average price: €8-20
Area: Friedrichshain
Address: Bänschstr. 41
10247 Berlin Germany
Phone: +49 30 42024943

#389
Piccolo Mondo
Cuisines: Italian
Average price: €21-40
Area: Charlottenburg
Address: Reichsstr. 9
14052 Berlin Germany
Phone: +49 30 30102030

#390
Miss Honeypenny
Cuisines: Bistro, Cafe
Average price: €8-20
Area: Schöneberg
Address: Winterfeldtstr. 44
10781 Berlin Germany
Phone: +49 30 22963533

#391
Restaurant Van-Long
Cuisines: Vietnamese, Thai
Average price: €21-40
Area: Mitte
Address: Reinhardtstr. 8
10117 Berlin Germany
Phone: +49 30 2823570

#392
Vietnam Village
Cuisines: Vietnamese
Average price: Under €7
Area: Prenzlauer Berg
Address: Oderberger Str. 7
10435 Berlin Germany
Phone: +49 30 36423292

#393
East London
Cuisines: British, Burgers
Average price: €8-20
Area: Kreuzberg
Address: Mehringdamm 33
10961 Berlin Germany
Phone: +49 30 69533205

#394
Da Piadina
Cuisines: Italian
Average price: Under €7
Area: Mitte
Address: Auguststraße 49A
10119 Berlin Germany
Phone: +49 30 54481948

#395
Otito
Cuisines: Asian Fusion,
Japanese, Vietnamese
Average price: €8-20
Area: Mitte
Address: Leipziger Str. 30
10117 Berlin Germany
Phone: +49 30 20605300

#396
Taverna Merkouri
Cuisines: Greek
Average price: €8-20
Area: Tiergarten
Address: Wiclefstr. 30
10551 Berlin Germany
Phone: +49 30 3956435

#397
Factory Girl!
Cuisines: Breakfast & Brunch
Average price: €8-20
Area: Mitte
Address: Auguststr. 29
10119 Berlin Germany
Phone: +49 30 33850062

#398
Kuchenkaiser
Cuisines: German, Desserts
Average price: €8-20
Area: Kreuzberg
Address: Oranienplatz 11-13
10999 Berlin Germany
Phone: +49 30 61402697

#399
Speisehaus
Cuisines: German
Average price: €8-20
Area: Friedrichshain
Address: Wühlischstr. 30
10245 Berlin Germany
Phone: +49 30 67968602

#400
Babel
Cuisines: Middle Eastern
Average price: €8-20
Area: Prenzlauer Berg
Address: Kastanienallee 33
10119 Berlin Germany
Phone: +49 30 44031318

#401
My Thais
Cuisines: Thai
Average price: Under €7
Area: Charlottenburg
Address: Krummestr. 35
10627 Berlin Germany
Phone: +49 30 31017010

#402
Kneipe Willy Bresch
Cuisines: German
Average price: Under €7
Area: Prenzlauer Berg
Address: Danziger Str. 120
10407 Berlin Germany
Phone: +49 30 4250905

#403
Ambar
Cuisines: Mexican
Average price: Under €7
Area: Tiergarten
Address: Bochumer Str. 5
10555 Berlin Germany
Phone: +49 30 39740915

#404
Olivenzweig
Cuisines: Delicatessen, Mediterranean
Average price: €8-20
Area: Weißensee
Address: Behaimstr. 14
13086 Berlin Germany
Phone: +49 30 92047696

#405
Café Pförtner
Cuisines: Cafe
Average price: Under €7
Area: Wedding
Address: Uferstraße 8-11
13357 Berlin Germany
Phone: +49 30 50369854

#406
Milchbart
Cuisines: Coffee & Tea
Average price: Under €7
Area: Prenzlauer Berg
Address: Paul-Robeson-Str. 6
10439 Berlin Germany
Phone: +49 30 66307755

#407
**Natürlicher Lebensraum
Kaffee & Kuchen**
Cuisines: Cafe
Average price: €8-20
Area: Tiergarten
Address: Jonasstr. 7
10551 Berlin Germany
Phone: +49 173 6327829

#408
Room 77
Cuisines: American, Mexican
Average price: €8-20
Area: Kreuzberg
Address: Graefestr. 77
10967 Berlin Germany
Phone: +49 30 3110-2260

#409
Kamala
Cuisines: Thai
Average price: €8-20
Area: Mitte
Address: Oranienburger Str. 69
10117 Berlin Germany
Phone: +49 30 2832797

#410
Habibi
Cuisines: Middle Eastern
Average price: Under €7
Area: Schöneberg
Address: Goltzstr. 24
10781 Berlin Germany
Phone: +49 30 2153332

#411
Gaststätte Walhalla
Cuisines: German
Average price: €8-20
Area: Tiergarten
Address: Essener Str. 8
10555 Berlin Germany
Phone: +49 30 3933039

#412
Café Moabit
Cuisines: Cafe
Average price: €8-20
Area: Tiergarten
Address: Emdener Str. 55
10551 Berlin Germany
Phone: +49 1522 6328010

#413
Falafel Salam
Cuisines: Middle Eastern
Average price: Under €7
Area: Wilmersdorf
Address: Rankestr. 3
10789 Berlin Germany
Phone: +49 30 8813461

#414
Petite Europe
Cuisines: Italian, Pizza
Average price: €8-20
Area: Schöneberg
Address: Langenscheidtstr. 1
10827 Berlin Germany
Phone: +49 30 7812964

#415
Lemongrass
Cuisines: Vietnamese
Average price: Under €7
Area: Charlottenburg
Address: Quedlinburger Str. 38-48
10589 Berlin Germany
Phone: +49 30 3309119698

#416
Daitokai
Cuisines: Japanese, Sushi Bar
Average price: Above €41
Area: Wilmersdorf
Address: Tauentzienstr. 9-12
10789 Berlin Germany
Phone: +49 30 2618090

#417
Happa-Happa
Cuisines: Cafe
Average price: €8-20
Area: Weißensee
Address: Smetanastr. 17
13088 Berlin Germany
Phone: +49 30 29045225

#418
Zsa Zsa Burger
Cuisines: Burgers, American
Average price: €8-20
Area: Schöneberg
Address: Motzstr. 28
10777 Berlin Germany
Phone: +49 30 21913470

#419
Viet Bowl
Cuisines: Asian Fusion, Vietnamese
Average price: Under €7
Area: Friedrichshain
Address: Straßmannstraße 41 Ecke
Ebertystraße, 10249 Berlin Germany
Phone: +49 30 42014942

#420
Lutter & Wegner
Cuisines: German, Wine Bar
Average price: €21-40
Area: Wilmersdorf
Address: Schlüterstr. 55
10629 Berlin Germany
Phone: +49 30 8813440

#421
Sisaket Thai Restaurant
Cuisines: Thai
Average price: €8-20
Area: Mitte
Address: Mauerstr. 76
10117 Berlin Germany
Phone: +49 30 20658186

#422
Latino
Cuisines: Italian
Average price: €8-20
Area: Charlottenburg
Address: Uhlandstr. 4
10623 Berlin Germany
Phone: +49 30 3124046

#423
**Rosenthaler Grill
und Schlemmerbuffet**
Cuisines: Turkish, Italian
Average price: Under €7
Area: Mitte
Address: Torstr. 125
10119 Berlin Germany
Phone: +49 30 2832153

#424
Creperie Manouche
Cuisines: Creperies
Average price: €8-20
Area: Kreuzberg
Address: Grimmstraße 23
10967 Berlin Germany
Phone: +49 30 83219319

#425
Rüan Thai Restaurant
Cuisines: Thai
Average price: €8-20
Area: Reinickendorf
Address: Brunowstr. 8
13507 Berlin Germany
Phone: +49 30 8542137

#426
Mae Charoen Thai Imbiss
Cuisines: Thai
Average price: Under €7
Area: Neukölln
Address: Sonnenallee 134
12059 Berlin Germany
Phone: +49 30 56829381

#427
Filetstück
Cuisines: German
Average price: €21-40
Area: Wilmersdorf
Address: Uhlandstraße 156
10719 Berlin Germany
Phone: +49 30 54469640

#428
Café Dazwischen
Cuisines: Breakfast & Brunch, Cafe
Average price: Under €7
Area: Wedding
Address: Torfstr. 16
13353 Berlin Germany
Phone: +49 30 34711117

#429
Hackbarths
Cuisines: Bar, German
Average price: Under €7
Area: Mitte
Address: Auguststr. 69a
10117 Berlin Germany
Phone: +49 30 2827704

#430
Gyros Express
Cuisines: Kebab
Average price: Under €7
Area: Neukölln
Address: Johannistaler Chaussee 264
12351 Berlin Germany
Phone: +49 30 6035556

#431
Ankerklause
Cuisines: Breakfast & Brunch
Average price: €8-20
Area: Kreuzberg
Address: Kottbusser Damm 104
10967 Berlin Germany
Phone: +49 30 6935649

#432
Mundo Restaurant Café Bar
Cuisines: Spanish, Mediterranean
Average price: €8-20
Area: Tempelhof
Address: Alt-Mariendorf 32
12107 Berlin Germany
Phone: +49 30 74079740

#433
Sagar
Cuisines: Indian
Average price: €8-20
Area: Wilmersdorf
Address: Prinzregentenstraße 53
10715 Berlin Germany
Phone: +49 30 85070094

#434
Krasselts Currywurst
Cuisines: Curry Sausage
Average price: €8-20
Area: Steglitz
Address: Steglitzer Damm 22
12169 Berlin Germany
Phone: +49 30 7969147

#435
Bier's im S-Bhf.
Cuisines: Curry Sausage
Average price: Under €7
Area: Mitte
Address: Friedrichstr. 141-142
10117 Berlin Germany
Phone: +49 30 20452158

#436
Arema
Cuisines: Cafe
Average price: €8-20
Area: Tiergarten
Address: Birkenstr. 30
10551 Berlin Germany
Phone: +49 30 50185736

#437
Tung Long Bistro
Cuisines: Vietnamese
Average price: Under €7
Area: Neukölln
Address: Karl-Marx-Str. 59
12043 Berlin Germany
Phone: +49 6290 0908

#438
OM
Cuisines: Indian
Average price: Under €7
Area: Tiergarten
Address: Kirchstr. 16
10557 Berlin Germany
Phone: +49 30 39749554

#439
Al Contadino Sotto Le Stelle
Cuisines: Italian
Average price: €21-40
Area: Mitte
Address: Auguststr. 36
10119 Berlin Germany
Phone: +49 30 2819023

#440
Marques
Cuisines: Mediterranean, Spanish
Average price: €21-40
Area: Kreuzberg
Address: Graefestr. 92
10967 Berlin Germany
Phone: +49 30 61625906

#441
Filetstück
Cuisines: Steakhouse
Average price: €21-40
Area: Prenzlauer Berg
Address: Schönhauser Allee 45
10435 Berlin Germany
Phone: +49 30 48820304

#442
Wild Caffè
Cuisines: Cafe, Bistro
Average price: €8-20
Area: Schöneberg
Address: Südwestkorso 63
12161 Berlin Germany
Phone: +49 30 48822648

#443
Burgerie
Cuisines: Burgers, Vegetarian
Average price: €8-20
Area: Prenzlauer Berg
Address: Schönhauser Allee 50
10437 Berlin Germany
Phone: +49 30 83212440

#444
Ye-Mc
Cuisines: Fast Food
Average price: Under €7
Area: Spandau
Address: Streitstr. 58
13587 Berlin Germany
Phone: +49 30 35306959

#445
Restaurant Ypsilon
Cuisines: Greek
Average price: €8-20
Area: Schöneberg
Address: Hauptstr. 163
10827 Berlin Germany
Phone: +49 30 7824539

#446
Les 3 Veuves
Cuisines: Burgers
Average price: €8-20
Area: Wilmersdorf
Address: Fechnerstr. 30
10717 Berlin Germany
Phone: +49 30 86008251

#447
Opatija-Grill
Cuisines: Serbo Croatian
Average price: €8-20
Area: Wedding
Address: Müllerstr. 70
13349 Berlin Germany
Phone: +49 30 4521016

#448
Ottenthal
Cuisines: Austrian
Average price: €21-40
Area: Charlottenburg
Address: Kantstr. 153
10623 Berlin Germany
Phone: +49 30 3133162

#449
Restaurant Scheune
Cuisines: German
Average price: €8-20
Area: Wilmersdorf
Address: Eichkampstr. 155
14055 Berlin Germany
Phone: +49 30 8924903

#450
12 Apostel
Cuisines: Italian, Pizza
Average price: €21-40
Area: Mitte
Address: Georgenstr. 2
10117 Berlin Germany
Phone: +49 30 2010222

#451
Schraders
Cuisines: Breakfast & Brunch,
Burgers, Tapas
Average price: €8-20
Area: Wedding
Address: Malplaquetstr. 16B
13347 Berlin Germany
Phone: +49 30 45082663

#452
Restaurant Savanna
Cuisines: African, Ethiopian
Average price: €21-40
Area: Prenzlauer Berg
Address: Sredzkistr. 26
10435 Berlin Germany
Phone: +49 30 44318621

#453
Caramel
Cuisines: Italian, Delicatessen
Average price: Under €7
Area: Kreuzberg
Address: Zimmerstr. 26
10969 Berlin Germany
Phone: +49 30 25931958

#454
Weder Gestern Noch Morgen
Cuisines: Cafe, Bistro
Average price: €8-20
Area: Friedrichshain
Address: Gärtnerstr. 22
10245 Berlin Germany
Phone: +49 30 89569615

#455
Gaststätte Artemis
Cuisines: Greek
Average price: €8-20
Area: Treptow
Address: Schnellerstr. 97
12439 Berlin Germany
Phone: +49 30 67822870

#456
Gaststätte Zur Haxe
Cuisines: German
Average price: €8-20
Area: Prenzlauer Berg
Address: Erich-Weinert-Str. 128
10409 Berlin Germany
Phone: +49 30 4216312

#457
Gusto Cucina Italiana
Cuisines: Italian
Average price: €8-20
Area: Wilmersdorf
Address: Bregenzer Straße 1
10707 Berlin Germany
Phone: +49 30 8836722

#458
Lemongrass
Cuisines: Thai, Asian Fusion
Average price: €8-20
Area: Friedrichshain
Address: Simon-Dach-Str. 2
10245 Berlin Germany
Phone: +49 30 20056975

#459
Cooking Papa
Cuisines: Korean
Average price: €8-20
Area: Wilmersdorf
Address: Wilmersdorfer Straße 72
10629 Berlin Germany
Phone: +49 30 95591586

#460
Parlamento Degli Angeli
Cuisines: Italian
Average price: €8-20
Area: Kreuzberg
Address: Bergmannstraße 109
10961 Berlin Germany
Phone: +49 30 81806400

#461
Masala
Cuisines: Indian
Average price: Under €7
Area: Köpenick
Address: Slabystr. 25
12459 Berlin Germany
Phone: +49 30 66636806

#462
Izumi
Cuisines: Sushi Bar, Japanese
Average price: €21-40
Area: Mitte
Address: Kronenstr. 66
10117 Berlin Germany
Phone: +49 30 20649938

#463
Cafe Rosenrot
Cuisines: Cafe
Average price: €8-20
Area: Pankow
Address: Ossietzkystr. 2a
13187 Berlin Germany
Phone: +49 30 54736759

#464
Reinhard's Restaurant
Cuisines: French, German
Average price: €21-40
Area: Mitte
Address: Poststr. 28
10178 Berlin Germany
Phone: +49 30 2425295

#465
Lemon Grass Scent
Cuisines: Asian Fusion
Average price: Under €7
Area: Prenzlauer Berg
Address: Schwedter Str. 12
10119 Berlin Germany
Phone: +49 30 40576985

#466
RisOtto
Cuisines: Italian
Average price: €8-20
Area: Mitte
Address: Friedrichstr. 115
10117 Berlin Germany
Phone: +49 173 7171626

#467
Umspannwerk Ost
Cuisines: German, International
Average price: €21-40
Area: Friedrichshain
Address: Palisadenstr. 48
10243 Berlin Germany
Phone: +49 30 42809497

#468
Kimchi Princess
Cuisines: Korean
Average price: €21-40
Area: Kreuzberg
Address: Skalitzerstr. 36
10999 Berlin Germany
Phone: +49 163 4580203

#469
Scheers Schnitzel
Cuisines: Bistro, Fast Food
Average price: Under €7
Area: Friedrichshain
Address: Warschauer Str.
10245 Berlin Germany
Phone: +49 1578 8948011

#470
Aki Tatsu
Cuisines: Japanese
Average price: €8-20
Area: Schöneberg
Address: Winterfeldtstraße 40
10781 Berlin Germany
Phone: +49 30 23607861

#471
Gaststätte Mendoza
Cuisines: Steakhouse
Average price: €8-20
Area: Charlottenburg
Address: Spandauer Damm 157
14050 Berlin Germany
Phone: +49 30 3051515

#472
Maharadscha
Cuisines: Indian, Vegetarian
Average price: €8-20
Area: Schöneberg
Address: Fuggerstr. 21
10777 Berlin Germany
Phone: +49 30 2138826

#473
Thai Huong
Cuisines: Vietnamese
Average price: Under €7
Area: Schöneberg
Address: Eisenacher Str. 54
10823 Berlin Germany
Phone: +49 30 78953472

#474
La Casa Buena Vista
Cuisines: Cuban, Cajun/Creole
Average price: €8-20
Area: Weißensee
Address: Bizetstraße 136
13088 Berlin Germany
Phone: +49 30 92370685

#475
Mesa
Cuisines: German
Average price: €21-40
Area: Tiergarten
Address: Marlene-Dietrich-Platz 2
10785 Berlin Germany
Phone: +49 30 25531572

#476
Tabibito Japan Restaurant
Cuisines: Japanese
Average price: €8-20
Area: Neukölln
Address: Karl-Marx-Str. 56
12043 Berlin Germany
Phone: +49 30 6241345

#477
3 Minutes Sur Mer
Cuisines: French
Average price: €21-40
Area: Mitte
Address: Torstr. 167
10115 Berlin Germany
Phone: +49 30 67302052

#478
Kvartira Nr. 62
Cuisines: Russian
Average price: €8-20
Area: Kreuzberg
Address: Lübbener Str. 18
10997 Berlin Germany
Phone: +49 179 1343343

#479
Sababa Restaurant
Cuisines: Mediterranean
Average price: €8-20
Area: Mitte
Address: 50-51 Kastanienallee
10119 Berlin Germany
Phone: +49 30 40505401

#480
Wirtshaus Heuberger
Cuisines: German
Average price: €8-20
Area: Schöneberg
Address: Gotenstr. 1
10829 Berlin Germany
Phone: +49 30 78957337

#481
Schwarze Pumpe
Cuisines: German, Breakfast & Brunch
Average price: Under €7
Area: Mitte
Address: Choriner Str. 76
10119 Berlin Germany
Phone: +49 30 4496939

#482
Machete
Cuisines: Mexican
Average price: €8-20
Area: Friedrichshain
Address: Neue Bahnhofstr. 29
10245 Berlin Germany
Phone: +49 30 32539868

#483
Seoul-Kwan
Cuisines: Korean
Average price: €8-20
Area: Schöneberg
Address: Schmiljanstr. 25
12161 Berlin Germany
Phone: +49 30 8526262

#484
Mabuhay
Cuisines: Indonesian
Average price: Under €7
Area: Kreuzberg
Address: Köthenerstr. 28
10963 Berlin Germany
Phone: +49 30 2651867

#485
Thalassa
Cuisines: Greek
Average price: €8-20
Area: Kreuzberg
Address: Gneisenaustr. 57
10961 Berlin Germany
Phone: +49 30 68817814

#486
Lon-Men
Cuisines: Chinese
Average price: €8-20
Area: Wilmersdorf
Address: Bamberger Str. 30
10779 Berlin Germany
Phone: +49 30 8545356

#487
Bötzow-Privat
Cuisines: German, Mediterranean
Average price: €8-20
Area: Mitte
Address: Linienstr. 113
10115 Berlin Germany
Phone: +49 30 28095390

#488
Cafe Chagall
Cuisines: Gastropub, Cafe
Average price: €8-20
Area: Prenzlauer Berg
Address: Kollwitzstr. 2
10405 Berlin Germany
Phone: +49 30 4415881

#489
Pastis
Cuisines: French
Average price: €21-40
Area: Wilmersdorf
Address: Rüdesheimer Str. 9
14197 Berlin Germany
Phone: +49 30 81055769

#490
Zur Kleinen Markthalle
Cuisines: German
Average price: €8-20
Area: Kreuzberg
Address: Legiendamm 32
10969 Berlin Germany
Phone: +49 30 6142356

#491
Schaumschläger
Cuisines: Coffee & Tea
Average price: €8-20
Area: Neukölln
Address: Hobrechtstr. 11
12047 Berlin Germany
Phone: +49 30 60902596

#492
Taverna Kos
Cuisines: Greek
Average price: €8-20
Area: Schöneberg
Address: Belziger Str. 68
10823 Berlin Germany
Phone: +49 30 7819413

#493
Einstein
Cuisines: Cafe
Average price: €21-40
Area: Mitte
Address: Unter den Linden 42
10117 Berlin Germany
Phone: +49 30 2043632

#494
Abirams
Cuisines: Indian
Average price: Under €7
Area: Kreuzberg
Address: Zossener Straße 12
10961 Berlin Germany
Phone: +49 30 69503103

#495
Pan
Cuisines: Breakfast & Brunch,
Vegetarian, Asian Fusion
Average price: €8-20
Area: Prenzlauer Berg
Address: Marienburger Str. 38
10405 Berlin Germany
Phone: +49 30 89392217

#496
Wok Show
Cuisines: Chinese
Average price: Under €7
Area: Prenzlauer Berg
Address: Greifenhagenerstr. 31
10437 Berlin Germany
Phone: +49 30 43911857

#497
Belmondo
Cuisines: French
Average price: €21-40
Area: Charlottenburg
Address: Knesebeckstr. 93
10623 Berlin Germany
Phone: +49 30 36287261

#498
Bombay
Cuisines: Indian, Cocktail Bar
Average price: €8-20
Area: Mitte
Address: Friedrichstr. 106
10117 Berlin Germany
Phone: +49 30 28484953

#499
Little Tibet
Cuisines: Asian Fusion
Average price: Under €7
Area: Kreuzberg
Address: Gneisenaustr. 6A
10961 Berlin Germany
Phone: +49 30 69004747

#500
Steakhaus Argentino
Cuisines: Steakhouse
Average price: €8-20
Area: Schöneberg
Address: Martin-Luther-Str. 103
10825 Berlin Germany
Phone: +49 30 7824023

Printed in Poland
by Amazon Fulfillment
Poland Sp. z o.o., Wrocław